W9-CCR-194

God's Call:
The Cornerstone of Effective Ministry

Neil Knierim and Yvonne Burrage

© Copyright 1997 • Convention Press
All rights reserved

ISBN: 0-7673-3467-1

Dewey Decimal Classification:
Subject Headings:
CHURCH VOCATIONS/VOCATIONAL GUIDANCE/
MINISTERS - CALL AND TRAINING

Unless otherwise noted, Scripture quotations are from the Holy Bible,
New International Version,
copyright © 1973, 1978, 1984 by International Bible Society.

Printed in the United States of America

Pastor-Staff Leadership Department
The Sunday School Board
of the Southern Baptist Convention
127 Ninth Avenue North
Nashville, Tennessee 37234

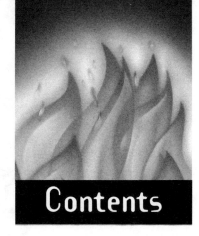

Contents

Introduction

Yvonne Burrage is a free-lance writer and teacher. She resides in Hendersonville, Tennessee.

Neil Knierim is a LeaderCare team leader and also church consultant for vocational guidance, LeaderCare Section, Pastor–Staff Leadership Department, Baptist Sunday School Board, Nashville, Tennessee.

This resource is designed to help you affirm that you have been called to vocational ministry. While it is true that every Christian is called to ministry, some are called to *the ministry*. These are persons who have determined that God wants them to serve Him through the vocation of ministry. They have sensed God calling them to the ministry, and they will express that calling in a variety of possible ways. While the expression may differ, the sense of calling is the key.

Each person pursuing the ministry must know for sure that he or she has been called to the ministry by God. This resource helps the reader examine that call and begin to consider the implications of this sense of call. The book is interactive in nature to help you work through your sense of call.

Once you have affirmed that God has called you to vocational ministry, this resource helps you consider how you are to live as a disciple of Christ moving toward vocational ministry. This is done in the second and third chapters of the book. Much of this information is borrowed from the book, *The Power of the Call*, by Henry Blackaby and Henry Brandt. These chapters focus on God's standard for your heart and God's standard for your ministry. It is important that you continue to grow in your relationship with Christ.

Before Paul discussed the work of the minister in 1 Timothy, he shared something of the character of the minister. To have credibility in your ministry, you must embrace the character of the minister. Becoming a spiritual leader is far more than a ministry position. It is embodying and demonstrating spiritual character and Christlikeness. Additional reading in this area should include the book, *Kingdom Leadership,* by Michael Miller.

Successful ministers need to understand God's call on their life, God's standard for their heart, and God's standard for their ministry. This resource is intended to help you get a good start in personalizing these things.

May God bless you as you follow His will for your life. And, may His will be better understood by working through this resource.

The Nature of Your Call

The ministry is not a profession you choose. God does the choosing. These words are important for anyone exploring the possibility of vocational ministry. God initiates the call to the ministry. We choose whether to respond by committing our lives to Him and His service or by selecting a different vocation. The ministry is not simply a vocational choice; it is a lifetime commitment.

A sense of call to the ministry is the cornerstone for an effective ministry. It is important that you know God has chosen you for vocational ministry. Some people are in the ministry for a variety of reasons. Some simply feel it would be nice to help people. Others just enjoy studying the Scriptures and teaching them to others. In some cases, they or their families have been helped by a minister or someone from a church and are so moved by this experience that they want to do the same for others. Still others may enter the ministry as a means of thanking God for saving them. They want to serve Him in this way as an expression of gratitude. These responses are all positive, but they are not the right responses.

Some pursue the ministry for less noble reasons. You will find ministers who surrendered to the ministry because a friend or relative did. They saw the affirmation their friend or brother received and were motivated to enter the ministry so they, too, could receive affirmation.

Many persons never have been affirmed for anything in their lives. They were unpopular in school, overlooked or overshadowed at home, and not readily accepted anywhere. But, when they walked down the aisle to surrender to the ministry, everything changed. They were received with open arms, affirmed, and respected. All of a sudden, by walking down the aisle of their church and saying they felt called to the ministry, they became "somebody."

Others see the ministry as a pretty good deal. You become a leader and have immediate respect. You have a great deal of freedom because you don't have to punch a time clock. The pay isn't bad, and you only have to work a couple of days a week. Not a bad deal.

Motivations such as these are poor and definitely not the right response to the ministry. The primary reason for committing your life to vocational ministry is because you have sensed this to be God's will for your life. Often accompanying this growing sense of call is the sense that you will not and cannot be satisfied doing anything else with your life. Let me try to define "call" and explain why it is essential.

Definition of "Call"

Often God's call to vocational ministry is a growing awareness that God has set your life aside for a special purpose of service for Him. I use the term *growing awareness* because oftentimes our sense of call gradually develops in our lives. Some people have a "Damascus Road" experience. They suddenly are stopped in their tracks; they know beyond a doubt that this is what their life is to be dedicated to; and that settles it.

However, the more common experience is a growing awareness that God is leading you further and higher, almost like a natural progression. You have experienced salvation. You have grown in your relationship with Christ. You have surrendered your life to Him and made Him the Lord of your life. Something inside you causes you to go further, to the point of saying, "God, whatever you want to do with my life, I am open and ready to follow you." Deep within, you gradually realize that the only satisfaction you will find is to surrender your life to Him and commit yourself to vocational ministry.

How you experience your call to the ministry is secondary to knowing you were called by God and not by friends, pastors, parents, or anyone else. Your call is a "God" thing. It doesn't matter if your call was a blinding light, a gradual process, or any experience in between. You know that God has put the motivation in your heart, mind, and soul to serve Him with your life through vocational ministry. At this point, in what role you will serve Him doesn't matter as much as the certainty that He has called you and you will dedicate your life to serving Him.

In your own words, define "call":

Testimonies of Sensing God's Call

Every kingdom leader has his or her own unique call. Times will come when a kingdom leader will need to return to the point of that call. "Did I really hear God call me?" "Is this what I should be doing?" "How do I get back to that excitement and blessing of answering God's call?"

Consider the following testimonies about experiencing God's call. Dr. Gene Mims, vice-president of the Church Growth Group of the Baptist Sunday School Board, vividly tells of the call he received from God at the age of 16. He was at home in Virginia, in his bedroom with earphones on, listening to rock 'n' roll on station WOWO out of Fort Wayne, Indiana, when he heard God tell him, "I want you to preach." Taking off his earphones, thinking that it was some funny "vibe" from the music, Mims waited. He again heard God's call: "I want you to preach." He never doubted his call to kingdom leadership from that moment on!

*   *   *   *   *

Reverend Al Gaspard also received a call from God as a teenager. While in high school, Al worked in the Louisiana rice fields. He was up at 2:30 a.m., sleepily driving the tractor, when he almost fell into the huge tractor disk, which would have killed him. The young man praised and thanked God for saving his life and was aware of God's presence with him. As he tells the event, you can hear the wonder in his voice: "I looked at the black dirt of the rice fields, and it had turned white. The Scripture came to me, 'the fields are white unto harvest.'" He plainly heard God say, "I want you to be a laborer!" By 6:00 a.m. he was beginning to doubt what had happened. For two weeks Al prayed about whether God wanted him to preach. Although he does not recommend following his example, he finally turned to God's Word and just opened the Bible. His Bible opened to Isaiah 52:7: "How beautiful on the mountains are the feet of those who bring good news, who proclaim peace, who bring good tidings, who proclaim salvation" (NIV).[1] Could there be any doubt now? Al did not answer that call but went on to college.

Al was married with two children, working at a hospital, and serving God as a lay member of his church when a friend asked him when he was going to give up his job and go to work for God. That night he prayed and asked God if He really did want him to preach. Like Gideon, Al asked God for a sign. "Lord, if You want me to preach, then ring a bell!" As Al and his family drove to church the next Wednesday night, the air conditioner on the car broke and the windows were rolled down. Out of nowhere a herd of cows blocked the road, and right in the middle of that herd was one big cow with a bell tied around her neck. That bell was ringing for Al! Finally, he said, "Yes, Lord, I'll preach!"

Reverend Gaspard has been preaching for 43 years as this testimony is being written! By the way, a friend went to the farmer and bought that bell for Reverend Gaspard. Times have come in his ministry when he has had to ring that bell and remind himself Who called him to kingdom leadership.

* * * * *

Bryan Lakey's (Associate Pastor of Pastoral Care and Ministries, First Baptist Church, Lakeland, Florida) voice fills with emotion and excitement as he tells of the call he received from God to full-time vocational ministry. God began working in Bryan's heart when he was 21 years old. "There was a question in my heart about whether I needed to be in the ministry." But, he never talked to anyone or followed through with that question. Four years later he still had the question in his heart, "Am I supposed to go into full-time ministry?"

For 17 years Bryan raised a family and worked in management at Mobil Oil. God didn't let go. While serving as an active member and teacher in the youth ministry of Calvary Baptist Church in Beaumont, Texas, God continued to touch Bryan's heart. He began to feel that his life held no eternal significance. Bryan began to have a desire in his heart to be useful to his family and to the family of God. Finally, he began to pray. He prayed for God to teach him to love people. The question came back, "Do I need to be in full-time vocational ministry?"

This time Brian prayed, searched the Scriptures, and sought counsel from godly men. His pastor, Dr. Claude Thomas, told him to "walk in as much light as God gives you." Bryan took that advice, read Scripture, attended revivals, and toured the seminary. Finally, one morning at 2:00 a.m., he had a sense of knowing he was called. "I must do this!" was his answer to God's call. Bryan quit his secular job, went to seminary, and worked full-time at First Baptist Church of Euliss, Texas, as the associate of administration. At first he thought he would be an administrator since he had so much experience in management from the secular world, but God had other plans. As time went on, Bryan realized that God had answered his prayer that he would have a love of people. He knew he was to work in pastoral care. His prayer now is to live a long life and give God back the 6,000 days it took him to answer the special call of God in his life.

How is God demonstrating patience with you in your life?

How does it encourage you to know that God does not give up on those He calls out to special ministry?

*   *   *   *   *

God calls each individual to a unique ministry. Doug Sarver has been called to be a minister of missions. He also was called out of the business world. Doug loved his successful restaurant business and couldn't believe God would call him to be a kingdom leader. God changed the desires of Doug's heart. As he served in his local church, he began to have a passion to serve, which overtook his passion for his work. He began to talk to his ministers and ask questions about full-time service. Doug was scared as he began to pray. Through sermons, godly counsel, and study of the Word, Doug began to understand that God was calling him. He woke up one morning and realized he no longer wanted to go to his beloved restaurant business. God had changed his heart and passion. At a men's retreat he was given a Scripture to read: "You are those who justify yourselves before men, but God knows your hearts. For what is highly esteemed among men is an abomination in the sight of God" (Luke 16:15, NKJV).[2] This was the confirmation! He knew he was being called by God into a special vocational ministry.

Write out a special Scripture that has ministered to you as you accept God's call in your life.

Each individual receives his or her call in a unique manner. God's call sometimes is easier to describe than to define. Let me share my sense of call with you.

I sensed God's call on my life when I was a junior in high school. I had grown up in church and was involved in every aspect of church life available to me. I was in Royal Ambassadors and the various choirs. I rarely missed Sunday School and Discipleship Training. I attended worship services regularly. As I entered the youth program at my church, I participated in everything. There were times when I was closer to the Lord than at others, but I tried to be what I should be as a Christian.

I had planned to pursue law as a vocation, and I began preparing myself through a variety of classes that were offered in high school. Early in my junior year, I sensed that maybe I should do something else with my life, but I was not certain what that might be. As the year moved on, I began to sense that maybe God wanted me to be a minister. What a revolting thought that was! I was fun loving, and most of the ministers I knew seemed a little stuffy. I did not think I would be happy being in the ministry if I had to be stuffy. The feeling about the ministry persisted until I had to talk to someone about it. I made an appointment with my pastor and went to his office to discuss the matter with him.

When I arrived, he greeted me warmly and invited me into his office. Before I had a chance to explain why I wanted to see him, he told me why I had come. He explained that he had sensed that God was calling me into the ministry for some time and that he was glad I finally had come to talk with him about it. I was shocked and affirmed at the same time. He knew about my call from God even before I told him. Only one more issue was left—the "stuffiness." I tried to explain that from what I had seen, I had far too much personality and zest for life to be a minister. I went on to explain that if I had to become stuffy to be a minister, then I wasn't sure I could. My pastor said something that was very important. He told me that God doesn't want to change us into somebody else or to change our personalities. He wants to refine us and use our uniqueness to glorify Himself. That settled for me any questions or doubts I had about my call to ministry in God's kingdom. I went forward during the invitation the following Sunday evening and committed my life to vocational ministry and announced my call to my church. As the members came by after the service to shake my hand, I was amazed when many of them mentioned that they had seen this coming for quite awhile. That evening was a great time of affirmation for my decision.

Two significant things stand out in my experience. One is that oftentimes others sense God's calling us to the ministry even before we sense it. The second is that God doesn't want to make us fit some certain pattern for our lives; He wants to celebrate the uniqueness of our personalities and lives, refine them, and use them for His glory. There are things that each of us can do and people we can impact because of who we are that others may never be able to do or to reach. Resist the temptation to try to be somebody else. Bring your life under God's authority, let Him refine who you are, and commit your uniqueness to Him. What a great concept!

Will your call to kingdom leadership be the same as others? Probably not. Each person's call is unique. Each ministry is unique. Your call is your call.

If you believe you have been called by God to be a kingdom leader, you need to express that call and your response to it in writing. What is your testimony regarding your call?

My Personal Testimony

Some points you might include in your testimony are:

1. The means God used to communicate with you (deep desire, dream, audible voice, blessed ministry, voice of a fellow Christian, God's Word, and so forth)
2. The personal circumstances of your life at the time of your call
3. The setting you were in
4. God's provisions to enable you to follow His call
5. Special Scripture promises
6. Fears
7. Steps you've taken to fulfill your call

Now, use the following space to write out your testimony of your call to vocational ministry. Include everything you can remember that has happened to bring you to this place. Be as detailed as possible.

Evaluate what you have written. Does what you have written indicate any of the wrong motivations for committing yourself to vocational ministry? Is it obvious that God has motivated this decision? Who was the greatest influence in helping you make this commitment?

Stop and ask God to really emblazon this experience on your heart. Ask Him to keep this sense of awareness fresh on your heart and in your mind. One of Satan's tools is to cause you to doubt that God has called you and set you aside for this purpose. A fresh awareness of God's call on your life will impact you and motivate you to impact your world for Christ.

Dealing with Doubt

Earlier I mentioned that one way Satan tries to stop us from impacting our world through vocational ministry is to cause us to doubt our call. If he can confuse us, we will pursue other things with our lives.

When I was in college, I experienced a time when I began to doubt my call to the ministry. I was uncertain about what I was to do. I was troubled because all the people back in the church where I grew up would be disappointed. The church had helped me financially with my education. I was confused and didn't want to face the issue because of the embarrassment it might cause. Finally, I had to deal with it and get it settled.

A revival team I was a part of had a revival scheduled a week away. I apologized to God about needing a visible sign that the ministry was where I should invest my life. I asked God to have at least one person come forward during the five days of the revival. I didn't tell anyone about the doubt I was experiencing because it was so personal and important to me. When the revival began I was nervous because of what was at stake for me. No one came forward the first service, second service, third, or fourth. After the fourth service, I got away by myself and simply poured out my heart before God. I explained that I wanted to know His will for my life and that it appeared I had misread what He had for me. I asked for help in getting through the last service of the revival and promised Him I never would preach again after that service if no one came forward. I had settled it and was ready to swallow my pride if it was clear that the ministry wasn't God's will for me.

I got through the service and offered the invitation. No one came during the first stanza of the invitation hymn. No one came during the second. I indicated to the music leader that we would sing one more stanza. Near the end of the last stanza, two women came forward. I was amazed. I had my answer. I thanked God for showing me His will and apologized for such a glaring lack of faith. I needed something visible and God provided. The next day back at college, I received word that 29 other people made decisions in the evening service as a direct result of the revival. I had my answer, and I had it clearly. This was where God wanted me to invest my life. Vocational ministry was God's clear plan for me.

This experience has been a cornerstone for me. Whenever I begin to doubt my call to the ministry, in my mind I go back to that Sunday morning in that revival service and see those two women walking down that aisle. Then I visualize the note from the pastor informing me of the additional decisions. The doubts are swept away by affirmation from God. I know beyond a doubt that this is God's plan for my life.

Everyone who commits to the ministry needs this type of assurance. It will keep you following God's plan for your life in the hard times that will come. The difficulties, the exhaustion, the frustrations, and the pains will be lessened when you realize that without a doubt, you are in the center of God's will. Satan will try to cause you to lose this focus. You may feel like walking away from the ministry; but, your sense of call will keep you there.

Reflect: Has there been a time when you doubted your call? Tell about it.

Refer to the section where you wrote out your experience of your call to the ministry. Make sure it is in as much detail as you can remember. Put down dates for as many events as you can remember. This will be the historical and emotional document that you can go back to if you begin to doubt your call. Were you sincere when you committed your life to vocational ministry? Was it with the right motivation? Reviewing your written testimony and answering these questions will help you stand in times of questioning. You may want to open your Bible to a blank cover page and copy this account of your call experience. Refer to it as often as necessary.

No Excuses

God has been calling out His children to kingdom leadership since Old Testament days. Men such as these received their calls in different ways:

- Abraham was called by God (Gen. 12:1–5);
- Ezekiel heard the word of the Lord (Ezek. 1:1, 3); and
- Peter, Andrew, James, and John were called by the Lord Jesus Himself (Matt. 4:18–22).

Often, though, when the call is heard, excuses about inability are offered to God. Moses immediately comes to mind as an example of this. God did not accept his excuse.

We are going to study Gideon's call. His call is found in the Book of Judges. The story took place in Israel's life in the promised land from the death of Joshua to the rise of the monarchy. The fundamental issue in the Book of Judges is the lordship of God in Israel. The fundamental issue for Gideon was the lordship of God. The fundamental issue for you as you listen to the call of God is the lordship of God in your life.

Read the following passages from Judges 6 (NIV) and answer the questions:

Judges 6:12:
When the angel of the Lord appeared to Gideon, he said, "The Lord is with you, mighty warrior."

Why did the angel of the Lord come to Gideon?

Judges 6:13:
"But sir," Gideon replied, "if the Lord is with us, why has all this happened to us? Where are all his wonders that our fathers told us about when they said, 'Did not the Lord bring us up out of Egypt?' But now the Lord has abandoned us and put us into the hand of Midian."

Circle all of the questions Gideon asked.
Gideon had doubts about whether the Lord was with him and with Israel. What were the causes of his doubts?

1.

2.

3.

Judges 6:14:
The Lord turned to him and said, "Go in the strength you have and save Israel out of Midian's hand. Am I not sending you?"

How did God encourage Gideon?

How has God encouraged you in your call?

"Go in the strength you have." How does this statement relate to your call and to the statement "you are a work in progress"?

Judges 6:15:
"But Lord," Gideon asked, "how can I save Israel? My clan is the weakest in Manasseh, and I am the least in my family."

What question did Gideon ask that showed his feelings of insecurity?

What question did Gideon ask that showed his worries about his family heritage?

What statement did Gideon make that showed his insecurity about his age?

Are there factors that make you feel insecure about your qualifications to accept God's call to kingdom leadership?

How does insecurity about God's call show a lack of faith?

Judges 6:16:
The Lord answered, "I will be with you, and you will strike down all the Midianites together."

Circle the encouraging answer God again gave Gideon.

Judges 6:17-23:
Gideon replied, "If now I have found favor in your eyes, give me a sign that it is really you talking to me. Please do not go away until I come back and bring my offering and set it before you."

And the Lord said, "I will wait until you return."

Gideon went in, prepared a young goat, and from an ephah of flour he made bread without yeast. Putting the meat in a basket and its broth in a pot, he brought them out and offered them to him under the oak.

The angel of God said to him, "Take the meat and the unleavened bread, place them on this rock, and pour out the broth." And Gideon did so. With the tip of the staff that was in his hand, the angel of the Lord touched the meat and the unleavened bread. Fire flared from the rock, consuming the meat and the bread. And the angel of the Lord disappeared. When Gideon realized that it was the angel of the Lord, he exclaimed, "Ah, Sovereign Lord! I have seen the angel of the Lord face to face!"

What was Gideon's request?

What miracle did the angel of the Lord perform?

How did Gideon respond?

What are the pros and cons about asking God for a sign?

Gideon continued to ask for signs from God (Judg. 6:24-40), and God patiently responded to Gideon's need. Finally, Gideon was faithful to obey and follow God's call to be a mighty warrior.

What can you learn from Gideon's story about God's patience, understanding, and perfect love for you?

Are there steps you need to take in faith to move forward with your call?

You may ask, "Why is it so important for people to sense that they are called by God to vocational ministry? This is an important question. If ministry were a business or other profession, it wouldn't matter. You could be a leader in any area through education and experience. You could develop the necessary skills to perform your assigned tasks. But vocational ministry is different. This work has a supernatural element. It cannot be done by just anyone; it must be done by those who are called and anointed by God.

In your own words explain why it is important to know you are called by God to vocational ministry.

Called Apart

As one called by God to vocational ministry, you have been anointed by Him for this role.—God has placed His hand on your life and has set you aside for His service. This is a very special calling—the highest calling. Just as God called and anointed Abraham, Moses, Joshua, the prophets, the judges, and the apostles, He has called and anointed you. What was there about Moses that caused the children of Israel to recognize that he was to lead them out of bondage into the promised land? What was there about Joshua that gave him the right to follow Moses' leadership and complete the task God had given to Moses? What was there about any of the leaders from the Old and New Testaments that caused them to impact their societies and people whose lives touched theirs? The answers are that each of them were anointed and called by God.

Paul tells us from the pages of his letters that he did not choose to be an apostle, but that God had chosen his ministry for him and anointed him to do the work. God's supernatural impact in our lives empowers us to do the work of the ministry effectively. Through *the call* you know beyond a doubt that this is what your life is to be about. Through *the anointing* others can see God's hand on you. This is why it is important for you to share your call with others and for them to recognize that God does have His hand on you. The greatest impact will be made with your life when you take God's call and anointing and combine them with spiritual maturity, education, experience, and the development of necessary skills to be the best and most usable vessel you can be.

A great difference exists between a person who has chosen to be a minister and one whom God has called to the ministry. The most noticeable difference is the absence of this anointing. This anointing is not a reason for pride but a commitment to humility and service.

Persons who are secure in God's call to vocational ministry have a quiet confidence in their lives.— This confidence comes from knowing that they are in the center of God's will. These persons know that their motives are pure and their intent is simply to give their lives to serving God and those for whom Jesus died. They are not trying to gain attention or fame; they simply are pursuing God's will for their lives. They offer themselves as living sacrifices, realizing that wherever God leads is where they want to go. Paul reflected this in his life as he moved from place to place, responding to God's leadership willingly and openly.

A third reason it is important for you to know that God has called you and that you have not simply chosen ministry as a profession is that you must realize you are not working for God but with Him.— There is an important difference. If I am working *for* God, then He simply needs to tell me what to do and I will do it. If I am working *with* God, then there is a constant realization that I am limited in what I can do in my own power and that every attempt must be made to do my work in His power. What does this mean? It means I realize I have limited wisdom but God is the author of wisdom. It means I have limits on my ability to love others but God is love. It means I can do certain things to help people but God is unlimited in His ability to bring healing and help into people's lives. When we realize that God is the One who empowers us to do vocational ministry, we are working with Him and not for Him. If I am doing vocational ministry because I chose it rather than because God chose it for me, I may not be as aware of the necessity of His empowerment in my ministry as I need to be.

Reflect: Explain in your own words the difference between working "for" God and working "with" Him. So far in your life, have you been working for or with God?

Recall: Name the three indicators that separate those who have been called by God into vocational ministry from those who simply have chosen ministry as a profession.

1.

2.

3.

The anointing of God on our lives, the quiet confidence of being in the center of His will for our lives, and the awareness of the need to work with God separate those who are called by God into vocational ministry from those who simply have chosen ministry as a profession. May you experience these three things in your life and ministry.

Limitations

Can I disqualify myself for vocational ministry? The answer, of course, is yes. God has set a standard of living for vocational ministers. Paul talked about those standards in his first letter to Timothy. In 1 Timothy 3–5, Paul explained the character, requirements, and work of the minister. The second section of this book, "Standards of the Spiritual Heart," deals with these standards. However, let me use the life of Samson to illustrate what happens when one whom God has His hand on limits how God can use him.

Samson was a judge whom God was using to bring judgment on the Philistines. The covenant God had with Samson was initiated even before Samson's birth. It was signified by his lifestyle and by the requirement that a razor would not touch his head.

As the story unfolds, Samson was experiencing great success in being used by God when his focus became hazy. He began to wonder if he might be missing something in life and looked to see what else might be out in the world. He knew he was being used by God and committed to His service, but he began to wander. He met Delilah, lost control of his life, and negatively impacted his ministry through a series of bad choices.

As you know from the account of this experience in the Bible, the Philistines paid Delilah to discover the source of Samson's strength and deliver him to them. Delilah asked Samson to tell her the source of his strength. Instead of fleeing, he decided to have a little fun.

In round 1 Samson told Delilah that if she tied him up in seven green cords, he would be powerless. He fell asleep, and she tied him in seven green cords and woke him up. He broke the cords as he awoke and continued to play with fire.

In round 2 when Delilah asked about the source of his strength again, rather than leave and salvage his ministry, he stayed. If he had left after the first incident, he could have continued in his role as a judge and done even greater things. But, he was fascinated with Delilah and the game they were playing, and he decided to play another round. This time, he said if he were tied in new ropes he would be powerless. He fell asleep, she tied him in new ropes, and woke him up. He broke loose again and continued to play the third round.

There is nothing of a disqualifying nature to Samson's calling and ministry yet. The danger was that he thought he could control the situation rather than it controlling him. He may have thought it was just a little fun with no consequences. But, there are consequences to the decisions we make. We must avoid situations that can impact our life and witness negatively. The consequence of self-reliance could be that we will disqualify ourselves from ministry.

Round 3 for Samson continued to be dangerous. This time he said the source of his power was related to his hair. He explained that if his hair were woven into seven locks he would be powerless. He fell asleep again, Delilah wove his hair into seven locks and waked him for the third time. He sprung up, winning round 3. Delilah explained that she was tired of being made fun of and that she was tired of playing games.

Round 4 was a disaster. Samson explained that he was a Nazirite and that he was committed to God even before he was born. He further explained that his hair was a symbol of his commitment and that if it were cut, he would lose his power. He fell asleep; she cut his hair; he was powerless; and he lost round 4 and the entire game. As he awoke, the Philistines captured him and rendered him useless. The great judge whom God was using had disqualified himself from service. He didn't mean to. He likely was only trying to have a little fun. He thought he was in control and he could stop the game when he wanted. But, Samson had put himself in a bad situation, refused to leave, and now was unable to be used by God.

Reflect: What was Samson's key problem?

Have you ever put yourself in a situation you thought you could control alone?

How can you avoid following in Samson's footsteps?

As one pursuing vocational ministry, you must be careful not to disqualify yourself from vocational ministry. Sure, some things may appear innocent at first; but many things have serious consequences. Watch your language, don't go to places where you don't belong, keep yourself pure in your relationships, be honorable in all your dealings with people, and be a person of character and integrity. You may be thinking, *Didn't Samson kill more Philistines at his death when God remembered him after he confessed and asked God to remember him?* The answer is yes, but God could have used him in even greater ways if he had kept his covenant with God and lived out his commitment. If you do something that would disqualify you, the opportunity to be restored to vocational ministry may not always be available. (Many sources of help are available; however, an emergency resource all pastor-church staff leaders and their families need to know about is the LeaderCare Hotline (1-888-789-1911) at the Baptist Sunday School Board. This service is available 24 hours a day, 7 days a week for those in need of help.)

Which Ministry?

"What if I don't know what I am being called to?" Don't worry if you don't know exactly how God wants to use you right now. Some people immediately know what kind of ministry God has for them, while others are uncertain. You may know that God wants to use you as a foreign missionary in a particular country and in a specific ministry role. The opposite of that may be that you don't know how God wants to use you but you do know He does want to use you in some place, at some time, in some way.

The key here is that you surrender yourself to whatever God might have for you, and with excitement and anticipation embark on the journey to find it. The dynamic factor at this point isn't where or how, but that you are making yourself available. Regardless of the time, place, or role, if you aren't open to His leadership and will, it won't matter. Your availability to serve, preparation, giftedness, abilities, sanctified life, and total being committed to God are the requirements. You may serve God in a number of places and in a variety of ministry positions, but your commitment to vocational ministry never changes.

I have served as a minister of youth, minister of education, associate pastor, pastor, state convention worker, and through the Baptist Sunday School Board. All of these roles have been expressions of my call to vocational ministry. Sometimes we get caught up in where and how. "What will I be when I grow up?" may be the question. The best answer is, "Whatever God leads me to be."

Your call to vocational ministry may take several forms of expression. You may be a youth minister your entire ministry. You may be a pastor your entire ministry. It's possible that you may serve as a church staff member, gain a great deal of experience in the work of the ministry and how the church operates, and eventually use that knowledge and experience to serve as a pastor.

I have written the following words on an inside page of my Bible. I refer to them from time to time. They read, "Begin by committing your whole life to God. Then, let Him lead you a step at a time." Don't answer the call to vocational ministry wondering how you will serve God through your ministry. If you know, thank Him for the clarity of your calling, but remain open to whatever might come your way in the years to come. God's will is not static; it is alive and sometimes involves changes in ministry roles. If you don't know exactly how God will use you, make it a matter of prayer. He will show you how He wants to use you. Get into the game, and He will reveal to you what position He wants you to play.

If you know what role God has for you in vocational ministry, write it down.

If you are uncertain, write a prayer in the following space, asking God to reveal to you the role He has for you. Commit to Him that even though you don't know how or in what kind of role you will serve Him, you are willing to trust Him for the answers.

"How can I prepare for vocational ministry?" This is an excellent question. There are at least five things that anyone at any stage in life can do to prepare for vocational ministry. These five things are appropriate if you are a teenager in junior or senior high school, a college student, or an adult who has sensed a call to the ministry. These five things are: (1) get an education, (2) continue to grow in your personal relationship with Christ, (3) get involved in a variety of ministry situations to gain valuable experience, (4) find a minister you respect to serve as your mentor, and (5) pray for God to reveal your ministry role to you. Each of these actions is important.

First, pursue a balanced, quality education.—If you are in junior or senior high school, continue to learn and do quality academic work. Consider pursuing a college and seminary education. These experiences will provide a solid foundation for your ministry.

If you are in college, continue to excel in your academics and look toward seminary for a theological education to complement your undergraduate degree.

As an adult established in a career, the decision is a little more involved. If you have an undergraduate degree, give consideration to pursuing theological training. Family responsibilities are a major consideration as you pursue your call to vocational ministry. If seminary seems unrealistic, explore programs like seminary extension or off-campus studies. If you don't have a college degree, consider taking classes through correspondence opportunities or on local college campuses. The six Southern Baptist seminaries also offer special training programs for persons without college degrees. Give serious consideration to preparing yourself academically.

Second, continue to grow in your personal relationship with Christ.—Develop your spiritual disciplines. Spend time in the Word of God. Develop a love and appreciation for Scripture. Read it devotionally and apply it to your life for refreshment and renewal. Study and memorize it to grow more familiar with the truths and promises of the Bible. Choose to live your life under the authority of this truth. Use Scripture to refine your life and show you how to live. Understand it and live it so you can preach and teach it with authority. Whatever expression your call to vocational ministry takes, the Bible will be central. The Holy Spirit will honor the time you spend in the Word by empowering you and your ministry. Develop a plan for spending time in prayer and worship with God. Learn how to pray and be diligent in your prayer time. Keep a journal of your requests and God's responses. Be an intercessor for others. Share your heart with God. Be still and listen for Him to lead and guide you. Don't miss the wonder of His presence and activity in your life. Be faithful in this area of your life.

Third, get involved in a variety of ministry situations to gain valuable experience.—Look for things to do at church. Volunteer to lead Bible studies. Work in Vacation Bible School. Go to a local nursing home and lead worship services. Learn how to witness and participate in visitation. Go on a mission trip. These are just a few of the ways you can begin now to experience ministry and to see God use your gifts and abilities.

Look for ways to develop leadership qualities. Tell your pastor, minister of music, youth minister, or other minister in your church that you would like to spend a day or two with them to observe their work and ministry style. They would be glad to help you understand what they do and allow you to observe. This hands-on approach will serve as important on-the-job training and will supplement the education you receive in college and seminary.

Fourth, find a minister whom you respect to serve as your mentor.—A lot of new experiences and questions are ahead of you as you pursue vocational ministry. These questions will relate to both personal issues and ministry matters. Finding someone who has walked the path you are beginning to follow will be invaluable. Think about a minister-pastor, youth minister, college minister, music minister, or some similar person for whom you have a great deal of respect and who might have the time and interest to help you begin your journey in vocational ministry. This person may be a college or seminary teacher. Select someone who could meet with you regularly, who is easy to talk to, and who demonstrates effectiveness in his or her personal life as well as ministry. Talk with this person about entering into such a relationship with you. Allow him or her to help you define what this relationship will become. The person simply may talk with you regularly or suggest books for you to read and then discuss them with you. Doing ministry together—observing the person and learning from him or her—also may be included. Develop the relationship jointly so that it will enrich your life and ministry.

Fifth, pray for God to open a ministry role for you.—For now, it might be a responsibility in a Sunday School class. It could be to be a summer missionary or a youth intern. Ask God to use these experiences to help you know what type of ministry role to pursue and prepare for. If you know, ask Him to affirm it to you. Involve others in praying for you. There are many possible ways God might choose to use you. Pray now that each one will be rewarding and significant as you seek to impact the world for Christ through your life and ministry.

Reflect: Evaluate the five preparation actions in your life right now. Under each action list the specific steps you are taking to develop the area:

1. Education

2. Growth in relationship with Christ

3. Ministry involvement

4. Mentor relationship

5. Prayer

1 From the Holy Bible, New International Version, copyright © 1973, 1978, 1984 by International Bible Society.
2 From the New King James Version. Copyright © 1979, 1980, 1982, Thomas Nelson, Inc., Publishers.

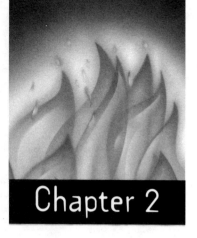

Chapter 2

Standards of the Spiritual Heart

As a man or woman who has received God's call, you are entering the most exciting, exhilarating journey of a lifetime. In order to maintain your sense of confidence and vitality in answering this call from God, you must continually evaluate your inner, spiritual life. As you serve Christ and His kingdom's work, ask yourself on a regular basis, "Am I where I should be?" This is not a vocational question, but a spiritual-maturity question.

In the book, *The Power of the Call* by Henry T. Blackaby and Henry Brandt, Brandt states, "If the minister is to be the one who can instruct God's people, he must maintain his own inner spiritual life with the Lord Jesus."[1]

This section of the workbook is designed for you to assess your maturity in various facets of the inner life. The activities are designed for you to interact with the book's content, with Scripture, and with God through prayer and the guidance of the Holy Spirit.

As you begin this section, take time to ask God to guide you and give you understanding about your call.

Maintain Your Heart
Read this passage from Deuteronomy 4:9 (NASB)[2]:

"Only give heed to yourself and keep your soul diligently, lest you forget the things which your eyes have seen, and lest they depart from your heart all the days of your life."

How do you give heed to yourself and keep your soul diligently?

What happens if a minister loses sight of his or her own spiritual character?

Rephrase Deuteronomy 4:9 as a personal response to God.

The Heart of the Called

When you receive and accept the call to ministry, you are giving your heart to God. What exactly does that mean? Persons today consider the heart the center of the emotions and intense feelings. Is that all you are giving to God? The Hebrew meaning of "heart" includes not only a person's feelings but also the spiritual, mental, and physical life of the individual. In other words, in the Hebrew context "heart" means the very focus of a person's life or, to put it another way, the core of a person's being. The Greek word for "heart" encompasses the center of both the spiritual and physical life. So, for this study, we'll define "heart" as the inner core of a person's total life: including mind, emotions, personality, and character.

In accordance with this definition, what is God seeking when He calls you to give Him your heart?

Read the following passage from Proverbs 4 (NASB) and write a paraphrase in the first person for this passage.

Verse 23: Watch over your heart with all diligence, for from it flow the springs of life.

Verse 24: Put away from you a deceitful mouth, and put devious lips far from you.

Verse 25: Let your eyes look directly ahead, and let your gaze be fixed straight in front of you.

Verse 26: Watch the path of your feet, and all your ways will be established.

Verse 27: Do not turn to the right nor to the left; turn your foot from evil.

My paraphrase:

Guard Your Heart

Basically there are three reasons to guard your heart. First, your heart is the source of your attitudes and actions. Second, your heart is the source of your words. The third reason to guard your heart is because your heart easily can be defiled and filled with wickedness.[3]

Mark the following Scripture references as to which reason they support for guarding your heart:

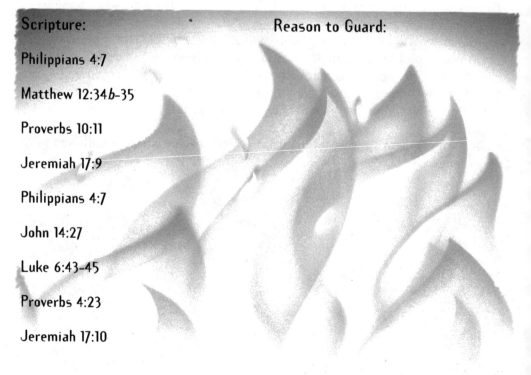

Scripture:	Reason to Guard:
Philippians 4:7	
Matthew 12:34b–35	
Proverbs 10:11	
Jeremiah 17:9	
Philippians 4:7	
John 14:27	
Luke 6:43–45	
Proverbs 4:23	
Jeremiah 17:10	

When God issues a call to ministry, He is issuing a tall order; this is not a call for those who are slackers in the faith. The apostle Paul set out the character qualifications of a minister in the church in 1 Timothy 3:1–7.

Read this passage and circle every character quality that Paul identified.

Here is a trustworthy saying: If anyone sets his heart on being an overseer, he desires a noble task. Now the overseer must be above reproach, the husband of but one wife, temperate, self-controlled, respectable, hospitable, able to teach, not given to drunkenness, not violent but gentle, not quarrelsome, not a lover of money. He must manage his own family well and see that his children obey him with proper respect. (If anyone does not know how to manage his own family, how can he take care of God's church?) He must not be a recent convert, or he may become conceited and fall under the same judgment as the devil. He must also have a good reputation with outsiders, so that he will not fall into disgrace and into the devil's trap (NIV). [4]

Using the Scriptures studied so far, compile a list of character qualities needed by a kingdom leader:

Personal Responsibility for the Heart

Consider this summary by Henry Blackaby from *The Power of the Call*. As you read, circle the word *heart*.

"The condition of our heart is in our hands and cannot be affected by things from the outside. We can 'stand guard over our heart,' keeping it with all diligence—because out of our heart flows our life. Good and evil things come from the heart. God examines the heart, knowing that good and evil things come from it. And the one God is looking for is the one whose heart is like His and His Son's. . . . We guard our heart by keeping a very close relationship with our Lord." [5]

List the daily activities you participate in that keep you in a close relationship with our Lord.

What kinds of things distract and pull you from a close relationship with the Lord?

In response to the above, are there any changes you need to make in your daily activities?

Explain your understanding of the following statement by Henry Blackaby: "This [close relationship with our Lord] is not merely a matter of maintaining a 'daily quiet time.'"[6]

A Heart Like Jesus'

To answer the call of God to become a leader in His kingdom work means much more than accepting church work as your vocation. You are not being called as a Christian technician, but as an extension, a representative, a co-worker with Jesus. To follow Jesus' example as the perfect leader, you must learn through a close relationship with Him. You are called to emulate His heart, which is also the heart of the Father (John 14:7).

Look up the following Scriptures and identify the heart qualities Jesus clarified and demonstrated:

1. John 11:33-35

2. Matthew 9:35-36

3. Matthew 9:12-14

4. Matthew 8:1-3

5. Luke 23:34

6. Philippians 2:5-7

7. John 10:14

8. John 13:14-17

9. John 15:10

10. John 15:12-17

Answers: (1) brokenness, (2) compassion, (3) concern, (4) willingness, (5) forgiveness, (6) humility, (7) self-sacrificing, (8) servant, (9) obedient, and (10) unconditional loving.

As you review these heart characteristics of Jesus, are there any areas you need to strengthen? List these and pray for the Holy Spirit to guide you into ways to strengthen these specific characteristics.

Not the World's Standards

Although leadership–management skills are useful, they cannot be the only skills used in kingdom leadership. The heart characteristics of Jesus are not the same leadership characteristics that the secular world seeks.

What character qualities do you think the secular world looks for in a leader?

How might business leaders evaluate the leadership qualities of Jesus?

Maintain a Clean Heart

In *The Power of the Call,* Henry Brandt stresses the importance of the pastor's (minister's) inner life:

"What goes on underneath your skin? You can come up to me and with a friendly smile, tell me how great you feel, even though you do not. You can act and look like a Christian and develop a pastoral manner so that nobody in the congregation would have a flicker of a hint that you are anything but a happy man. I hope that is not your goal. Watch yourself closely." [7]

In other words, you do not want to act as if you have the heart of Christ; you want to have it.

Know this: The heart is a deceitful thing. Our natural heart is not like the heart of Jesus. Jesus said it this way:

"And this is the condemnation, that the light has come into the world, and men loved darkness rather than light because their deeds were evil. For everyone practicing evil hates the light and does not come to the light, lest his deeds should be exposed" (John 3:19–20, NKJV).[8]

Circle the word *darkness* or any synonym referring to darkness in verses 19–20.

Consider any dark areas in your life. Read the following Scriptures and identify the "dark" actions of the sin-controlled nature.

- Colossians 3:5-9

- 1 Corinthians 6:18

- 2 Corinthians 5:16

- 2 Corinthians 6:3

- Galatians 5:19-21

Review the list you have just written and circle any "dark" areas that can be found in your life.

Confession Is a Constant

There is no human remedy for sin. Only Jesus died to save us from our sins. Only the Holy Spirit enables us to walk in the Spirit.

Read 1 John 1:8-9 (NIV):
If we claim to be without sin, we deceive ourselves and the truth is not in us. If we confess our sins, he is faithful and just and will forgive us our sins and purify us from all unrighteousness.

Take time now to confess any sins you found in your life as you circled actions on the sin-controlled nature list.

According to 1 John 1:8-9, what have you received after confessing your sins?

NOTE: This confessing of sins is *not* a one-time event! It is a continuing part of the close relationship with Jesus and the walk in the Spirit.

Experience Is Not the Answer

As a person seeking to answer God's special call, you will experience Satan's deceitful attacks. One of the clever ways Satan tempts is by convincing you that you can relate to others (the unsaved) only by experiencing what they experience.

This is a bold lie! Listen to how Henry Blackaby (in *The Power of the Call*) addresses this:

Sometimes people wonder how you can understand if you have not experienced what they have gone through. Have you ever stopped to think of what kind of training that would take? Why, you would need to be a thief, and a liar, and an adulterer. You would need to be divorced. You would need to beat up somebody. Would that be a strange course? [9]

Can you think of an experience when you have observed or participated in the above reasoning? If so, when and how?

Steps to Character Growth

Carefully read 2 Peter 1:3-11 (NIV):

His divine power has given us everything we need for life and godliness through our knowledge of him who called us by his own glory and goodness. Through these he has given us his very great and precious promises, so that through them you may participate in the divine nature and escape the corruption in the world caused by evil desires.

For this very reason, make every effort to add to your faith goodness; and to goodness, knowledge; and to knowledge, self-control; and to self-control, perseverance; and to perseverance, godliness; and to godliness, brotherly kindness; and to brotherly kindness, love. For if you possess these qualities in increasing measure, they will keep you from being ineffective and unproductive in your knowledge of our Lord Jesus Christ. But if anyone does not have them, he is nearsighted and blind, and has forgotten that he has been cleansed from his past sins.

Therefore, my brothers, be all the more eager to make your calling and election sure. For if you do these things, you will never fall, and you will receive a rich welcome into the eternal kingdom of our Lord and Savior Jesus Christ.

Complete the following review of this Scripture by filling in the blanks:

1. _____ enables you to live the Christian life.

2. God has made available all that you need for life and godliness through _____.

3. As a believer you are responsible to make every _____ to grow spiritually.

4. List the character qualities that produce a fruitful Christian life:

_____   _____

_____   _____

_____   _____

_____   _____

5. If you continue to grow in these qualities, they will keep you from being _____ and _____.

6. Be eager to make your _____ sure.

Reread 2 Peter 1:10 (NIV):
Therefore, my brothers, be all the more eager to make your calling and election sure.

Which of the following will assure you of your calling? Check all that apply.

a. Accepting personal responsibility for my spiritual growth

b. Growing in my knowledge of Jesus

c. Personal growth in spiritual qualities such as faith, goodness, self-control

d. Obeying God's Word

e. Learning through the life experiences that God provides for me

(Answer: Yes, all of the above will assure you of your call.)

Read this commentary on 2 Peter 1:5-9:
   "The 'adding' of a series of disciplines referred to by Peter describes the Christian's walk and growth in Christ. The power to accomplish these disciplines is provided through Jesus Christ. But the process of actually accomplishing them is determined by each Christian's attitude or response to the dealings of God in his or her life."[10]

Name a character-building circumstance that God has provided for you.

What character qualities were strengthened or are being strengthened in the circumstance God provided for you?

From what you have learned in 2 Peter 1, write a prayer response to God regarding making your calling sure.

Walk in the Spirit

The minister must realize that the condition of his or her heart does not depend on people or on life's circumstances. People and circumstances reveal the conditions of the heart. For example, when the bad driver cuts you off in traffic and you get angry, the bad driver's actions released the anger already present in your heart.

Your relationship to God will open up an insight into the condition of your heart, and your dependence on God is revealed through the people and circumstances He allows in your life.

Only a life yielded to the Spirit can be fruitful. The Bible says:

So I say, live by the Spirit, and you will not gratify the desires of the sinful nature (Gal. 5:16, NIV).

But the fruit of the Spirit is love, joy, peace, patience, kindness, goodness, faithfulness, gentleness, and self-control. Against such things there is no law (Gal. 5:22–23, NIV).

When people or life's circumstances do not reveal the fruits of the Spirit in your life, then you are not walking in the Spirit.

Do you agree or disagree with this statement? Explain.

Answer this question by checking the appropriate yes or no column. Do the people in your life now see the fruits of the Spirit as present and real in your daily life?

Fruit of the Spirit	Yes	No
love		
joy		
peace		
long-suffering		
kindness		
goodness		
faithfulness		
gentleness		
self-control		

Explain how you can develop these fruits in your life.

Review by completing this statement:

Having the fruits of the Spirit in my life does not depend on _____ or life's _____.

In Summary
Think of your life and answered call to ministry as a tree. What does it take for your tree to produce fruit and to cast a shadow?

[1] Henry T. Blackaby and Henry Brandt with Kerry L. Skinner, *The Power of the Call* (Nashville: Broadman & Holman Publishers, 1997), 109–10

[2] From the New American Standard Bible. © The Lockman Foundation, 1960, 1962, 1963, 1968, 1971, 1972, 1973, 1975, 1977. Used by permission.

[3] Frank Damazio, *The Making of a Leader* (Portland, OR: Bible Temple Publishing, 1988), 71–72.

[4] From the Holy Bible, New International Version, copyright © 1973, 1978, 1984 by International Bible Society.

[5] Blackaby, 121–22.

[6] Ibid., 124.

[7] Ibid., 112.

[8] From the New King James Version. Copyright © 1979, 1980, 1982, Thomas Nelson, Inc., Publishers.

[9] Blackaby, 114.

[10] Damazio, 110.

Chapter 3

Standards of Spiritual Leadership

As a person who has received God's call to the ministry, you are accepting the responsibility to be a manager of God's possessions; God alone is the supreme Leader of His Kingdom. This unit is designed to help you assess your spiritual leadership skills and to examine Jesus' leadership example. As you interact with the content and Scripture, ask God to guide you through the work of His Holy Spirit.

In the book, *The Power of the Call,* Henry Blackaby sets the spiritual leadership standards in chapter 13, "Marks of Spiritual Leadership." As you begin this unit, read the quotes from Blackaby's chapter, answer the questions, and complete the personal responses.

Quote 1: "As I searched through the Scripture seeking to understand what God is looking for in the one He can use, I began to sense God does not look for 'leaders,' but rather for those 'whose heart is loyal to Him' (2 Chron. 16:9)."[1]

Question: In light of this quote, what is the leadership difference between King Saul and King David?

Response: Do you ever find yourself as a "King Saul"? Explain.

Do you need to make any changes so that you can be a "King David"?

Quote 2: "Certainly the supreme example of this {heart} is Jesus, of whom it was said, 'and, once made perfect, he became the source of eternal salvation for all who obey him' (Heb. 5:9, NIV). {He} was 'shaped' or 'made' by the Father into exactly the One He was looking for to redeem a lost world."[2]

Question: What are some events in Jesus' life that helped to "shape" His heart?

Respond: Identify one event in Jesus' life that points to the kind of leader you wish to become.

Quote 3: A person God uses is shaped by God, "as a potter shapes the clay into the very vessel He needs to accomplish His purposes."[3]

Question: What are some ways God has begun to shape you into the very vessel He needs to accomplish His purposes?

Respond: Write a commitment prayer to God acknowledging to Him the circumstances that are shaping you into His vessel.

Quote 4: God may select a person as His servant to help the people respond to Him as He leads them. "This servant is a 'worker together with God'" (2 Cor. 6:1).[4]

Question: What do you see as your role in being a "worker together with God"?

Respond: Are there changes you need to make in order to be God's servant leader?

Quote 5: "Preeminently the Lord looks for one whose heart 'is loyal to Him' (2 Chron. 16:9). This is a man after God's own heart! Character precedes assignment, determines assignment, and maintains assignment."[5]

Question: What are you doing to develop your Christian character?

Respond: Write your definition of a spiritual leader in the kingdom of God.

Biblical Examples of Spiritual Leaders

God has used many leaders in the Bible. These men and women demonstrated leadership qualities that God used and still uses. There are too many leadership qualities to study them all at this time since this study is focusing on those qualities that need to be developed as you begin your ministry. Read the following Scriptures and identify the leadership qualities that still are needed in the kingdom work today.

Scripture	Bible Character	Leadership Quality
1. Exodus 33:15	Moses	
2. Joshua 5:14	Joshua	
3. 1 Samuel 2:12-26	Samuel	
4. Daniel 6:3-5	Daniel	
5. Daniel 6:10-11	Daniel	
6. Numbers 27:15-21	Joshua	
7. 1 Samuel 17:47	David	
8. 2 Kings 2:1-2	Elisha	
9. Acts 11:1-18	Peter	
10. Galatians 1:11-24	Paul	

Answers: (1) Moses sought the presence of God before he tried to lead; (2) Joshua had great reverence for the Lord which led to a total submissive, servant heart; (3) Samuel grew in spiritual knowledge and in his ability to relate to others; (4) Daniel demonstrated a trustworthy integrity in his faithfulness to God and in his work; (5) Daniel remained in a constant state of prayer; (6) Joshua learned to accept responsibility gradually; (7) David recognized the sovereign leadership of God in the middle of success; (8) in Elisha, we see a loyal commitment to the man who was in authority over him; (9) Peter put his past mistakes behind him and demonstrated a teachable spirit; and (10) Paul spent 10 years in preparation for his missionary/preaching ministry.

As you prepare for and begin your ministry, always remember that your calling is a result of your relationship with the Lord. Keep your focus on God and grow in your knowledge and experience. Beware of spiritual pride; if you are going to compare your accomplishments, spiritual maturity, and calling, then compare them to Jesus' accomplishments, maturity, and calling!

Jesus, the Perfect Leader

God placed Jesus as the Leader of His people. In Him we find the clearest example of a leader who has a perfect relationship with the Father and is in perfect submission to the Father.

Henry Blackaby in *The Power of the Call* points to John 17 as "a plumbline for your leadership 'style.'"[6] He explains that John 17 looks at spiritual leadership from two perspectives: from God's and from man's perspective on what God does to show those He has chosen how to guide His people. As our spiritual leader Jesus points us to two relationships: His relationship to the Father who sent Him and His relationship to those God gave Him. These two relationships will be crucial relationships in your called ministry.

Marks of a Spiritual Leader

This part of the study will examine the leadership qualities that Jesus demonstrates in John 17. As you study this passage, remember to look at the two relationships: Jesus' relationship to the Father and His relationship to those God gave Him. Read the Scripture (NIV) and answer the questions that follow.

Mark №1: A Spiritual Leader's Goal

Read John 17:1: After Jesus said this, he looked toward heaven and prayed: "Father, the time has come. Glorify your Son, that your Son may glorify you."

What was Jesus' goal?

Following Jesus' example, write your own personal goal as a servant leader.

Mark №2: A Spiritual Leader's Credentials

Read John 17:2: For you granted him authority over all people that he might give eternal life to all those you have given him.

Jesus received His authority from whom?

Who alone can grant you all you need to fully represent Jesus and carry out His kingdom's work?

Mark №3: A Spiritual Leader's Assignment

Read the following Scriptures and identify the assignment given and to whom:

Scripture:	Assignment:	Servant Leader:
1. John 17:2		
2. Matthew 28:19		
3. Matthew 28:20		
4. Acts 1:8		
5. Colossians 1:27-29		

Answers: (1) Giving eternal life, (2) making disciples, (3) teaching Jesus' commands, (4) presenting people perfect in Christ, and (5) being Jesus' witnesses.

As a disciple, as one who has answered the call to be set apart to work in the Father's kingdom work, summarize in your own words the spiritual leader's assignment:

Write a prayer to God accepting the spiritual leader's assignment.

A suggestion from Dr. Blackaby: "It would be very helpful to read through the New Testament and make a list of all the commands of Jesus. Then begin to teach the people of God to practice everything you find."[7]

What steps would you have to take to complete this assignment?

How would a review of Jesus' commands focus your ministry assignment?

Mark №4: A Spiritual Leader's Passion

Read John 17:4: I have brought you glory on earth by completing the work you gave me to do.

How did Jesus bring the Father glory?

List some of the tasks that Jesus completed on earth.

How does Jesus' investment of three and one-half years of instruction to the disciples reflect His passion for the salvation of the world?

What is your passion?

What kind of time investment are you willing to make in others' lives?

Mark №5: A Spiritual Leader's Focus

Read John 17:6a: I have revealed you to those whom you gave me out of the world.

Also read John 14:5-11.

How did the disciples know the Father?

How do you know the Father?

Reflect on this quote by Henry Blackaby from *The Power of the Call*: "No leader can possibly lead where he has not been, or share what he has not knowingly experienced. The disciples came to know God by observing and practicing everything Jesus commanded. And this is how those we lead will come to 'know the Father and His Son.'"[8]

In your own words explain this principle of shared experience.

Mark №6: A Spiritual Leader's Stewardship

Read John 17:6b: They were yours; you gave them to me and they have obeyed your word.

Jesus acknowledged that all of His followers really belonged to whom?

How does this knowledge that all people are God's possessions whom He entrusts to His ministers affect your attitude toward those to whom you will minister?

Mark №7: A Spiritual Leader's Resources

Read John 17:7: Now they know that everything you have given me comes from you.

What were some of the resources God had given to Jesus?

(Possible answers: authority, power, words, the fullness of His Spirit, love)

The disciples knew clearly that these resources came from whom?

Read Acts 1:8. What resource does Jesus promise to His followers?

Explain how you know the resources of God are present in and through your life.

Mark №8: A Spiritual Leader's Teaching Heart

Read John 17:8: For I gave them the words you gave me and they accepted them. They knew with certainty that I came from you, and they believed that you sent me.

Jesus received words from _____ and gave them to
_____.

Circle the three verbs that describe the disciples' actions as Jesus gave them the word of the Father.

There is a cycle to be followed as you teach: Receive, know, and believe.

Jesus taught the disciples until they believed what about Him?

Read about Paul's teaching heart in Colossians 1:25-28.

What was Paul's commission?

What is the commission God has given to you?

Mark №9: A Spiritual Leader's Prayer Focus

Read John 17:9: I pray for them. I am not praying for the world, but for those you have given me, for they are yours.

Circle the words that tell for whom Jesus is praying.

Read Luke 22:32, John 17:15, and Romans 8:34.

To follow Jesus' example in these Scriptures, where will your prayer focus be?

Mark №10: A Spiritual Leader's Reputation

Read John 17:10: All I have is yours, and all you have is mine. And glory has come to me through them.

How is Jesus glorified?

Dr. Blackaby puts it this way: "The lives of the disciples, living out in their lives what Jesus taught, and His very life - in them - was what 'glorified' Jesus." [9]

A minister's life and teaching is reflected in the lives of those he is leading.

What is the impact of this statement on your view of personal reputation?

To what extent does Jesus' reputation depend on you?

Mark №11: A Spiritual Leader's Investment

Read John 17:11a: I will remain in the world no longer, but they are still in the world, and I am coming to you.

When Jesus left the world, who was left to continue God's redemptive work?

Jesus taught the disciples both in words and by example, and He prayed for them.

As a kingdom leader, how will you follow Jesus' example and invest in the lives of those entrusted to you?

Mark №12: A Spiritual Leader's Success

Read John 17:11b: Holy Father, protect them by the power of your name—the name you gave me—so that they may be one as we are one.

Jesus states His same desire in John 6:39: This is the will of him who sent me, that I shall lose none of all that he has given me, but raise them up at the last day (NIV).

In other words, Jesus did not want to lose any who had been entrusted to Him. His desire was that the disciples would continue in a full relationship with God—the Father, the Son, and the Holy Spirit.

In terms of what you have encountered in John 17, which is more important in your ministry—the number of people you lead or the spiritual maturity of those you lead?

Mark №13: A Spiritual Leader's Joy

Read John 17:11b: So that they may be one as we are one.

Jesus desired His disciples to have the "oneness," the relationship that He, the Father, and the Spirit had.

Read John 17:13: I am coming to you now, but I say these things while I am still in the world, so that they may have the full measure of my joy within them.

Read John 15:11: I have told you this so that my joy may be in you and that your joy may be complete.

Circle the words that describe Jesus' desires for His disciples.

As a kingdom leader, what should bring you the greatest joy?

Mark №14: A Spiritual Leader's Strategy

Read John 17:14a: I have given them your word.

Read John 15:15b: Instead I have called you friends, for everything that I learned from my Father I have made known to you.

John 14:10b: The words I say to you are not just my own. Rather, it is the Father, living in me, who is doing his work.

Circle all of the nouns and pronouns that refer to God, the Father. According to these Scriptures, what was Jesus' strategy for teaching His disciples?

As a kingdom leader, who will be the source of your work and words?

Mark №15: A Spiritual Leader's Burden

Read John 17:14b: And the world has hated them, for they are not of the world any more that I am of the world.

What did Jesus know His followers would face?

As a kingdom leader, how will you prepare to face the world's opposition?

Mark №16: A Spiritual Leader's Prayer

Read John 17:15: My prayer is not that you take them out of the world but that you protect them from the evil one.

Jesus prays the same request in Matthew 6:13: *And lead us not into temptation, but deliver us from the evil one* (NIV).

How would the disciples know how to face the evil one?

How does Satan react when believers are close to God and resist the evil one?

Mark №17: A Spiritual Leader's Assurance

Read John 17:17: Sanctify them by the truth; your word is truth.

Jesus knew that God's Word is _____.

Jesus knew that God's Word would sanctify His disciples. In your own words define "sanctify."

The people you will encounter in your ministry do not need your word; they need _____'s word.

Read Isaiah 55:8-13. How does this Scripture encourage you as you are set apart to do His special work?

Mark №18: A Spiritual Leader's Mandate

Read John 17:18: As you sent me into the world, I have sent them into the world.

Jesus' mission sets the pattern for all who are called to minister. What is the mission you are to follow?

A spiritual leader must first know fully the sending of the Father in his own life. Then he must repeat the process in the lives of those entrusted to him.

Put the following steps in the correct order:
___ Faithfully "send them into the world."
___ Prepare them by diligent, thorough teaching and enabling.
___ Know when the Father has completed their equipping (Matt.16:15-27).
___Prepare them by an intimate, real, deep relationship with God.

(The correct order is: 4, 1, 3, and 2.)

Mark №19: A Spiritual Leader's Sensitivity

Read John 17:19: For them I sanctify myself, that they too may be truly sanctified.

Jesus set Himself apart to do God's will in order that His disciples also would_____

Jesus set the example in His own life. The disciples knew (and we know) by being with Jesus:
1. The Father had sent Him into the world.
2. The Holy Spirit had filled Him.
3. The Father's Word directed Him.
4. The Father was with Him.
5. He always pleased (obeyed) the Father.
6. God redeemed (saved) people through Him.
7. Nothing deterred Him.
8. He was "complete" in every way, and God reconciled the world to Himself through Him and in those who would obey Him.

Write down the eight factors you know about Jesus and will pass on to those entrusted to your ministry:

1.

2.

3.

4.

5.

6.

7.

8.

Do you see this pattern being fulfilled in your life? Explain.

Mark №20: A Spiritual Leader's Long-Term Kingdom View

Read John 17:20: My prayer is not for them alone. I pray also for those who will believe in me through their message.

1. Whom did Jesus include in His prayer?

2. What was His desire for all who believed in Him?

3. What did Jesus see as the result of the unity of all believers ?

As you accept the call to ministry, what is your long-term view of your mission?

Mark №21: A Spiritual Leader's Kingdom View

Read John 17:21: May they also be in us so that the world may believe that you have sent me.

List God's five-step plan:

1. God in_____.

2. Christ in_____.

3. Christ in the_____.

4. The disciples in_____.

5. The_____would believe.

Explain the importance of the quote, "fullness of God in a kingdom leader."

Mark №22: A Spiritual Leader's Gift

Read John 17:22: I have given them the glory that you gave me, that they may be one as we are one.

God gave Jesus His Glory, that is, the full presence of God expressed openly in and through His life.

What, then, does Jesus give to His followers?

You cannot give what you do not have. In order for you to pass on the glory of Jesus to those entrusted in your care, you need what?

Write a response to God regarding this statement: God's people long to see in their leader the life they long for themselves.

Mark №23: A Spiritual Leader's Union

Read John 17:23: I in them and you in me. May they be brought to complete unity to let the world know that you sent me and have loved them even as you have loved me.

All the fullness of _____ dwells in _____.

What is the result of unity—the fullness of God?

Here is God's plan and purpose. Put these sentences in the correct order.

___ God sent Jesus.

___ God loves His people as He loved His Son.

___ This relationship is available to all who will believe.

1 - 2 -3! God's plan and purpose and strategy to bring a lost world to Himself: God-in Christ-in His people.

How do you see yourself fitting into this union?

Mark №24: A Spiritual Leader's Desire

Read John 17:24: Father, I want those you have given me to be with me where I am, and to see my glory, the glory you have given me because you loved me before the creation of the world.

What two things did Jesus want for His followers?

Why did Jesus receive His glory?

A true spiritual leader's concern for those entrusted to him always will stem from what?

Mark №25: A Spiritual Leader's Satisfaction

Read John 17:25: Righteous Father, though the world does not know you, I know you, and they know that you have sent me.

As Jesus begins to close His prayer concerning His disciples, He states that although the world does not know God, He takes satisfaction in two things:

1.

2.

Why are the disciples a source of contentment for Jesus? What does He know they will do in His physical absence?

Will you be a source of contentment for Jesus? Why?

Mark №26: A Spiritual Leader's Completeness

Read John 17:26: I have made you known to them, and will continue to make you known in order that the love you have for me may be in them and that I myself may be in them.

In your own words summarize Jesus' conclusion to this prayer.

Read 2 Corinthians 5:14-15: For Christ's love compels us, because we are convinced that one died for all, and therefore all died. And he died for all, that those who live should no longer live for themselves but for him who died for them and was raised again (NIV).

Explain what the love of Christ is compelling you to do.

A Time of Preparation

You obviously are sincere and serious about accepting God's call to the ministry since you are completing this workbook. A desire to become a leader in God's kingdom work is not enough. Studying the perfect example of Jesus and His spiritual leadership qualities are not enough. You must be willing to submit to the preparing hand of God. Spiritual maturity and leadership does not happen by chance. God works to prepare you to become a kingdom leader.

God will bring people and circumstances into your life to accomplish these three things:
1. to strengthen your assurance of His call;
2. to lead you to examine your heart, motives, and attitudes toward ministry; and
3. to refine and mature you spiritually.

Look up the following Scriptures. Identify the God-called leader and the principle God used as preparation for the kingdom task God would call each one to complete.

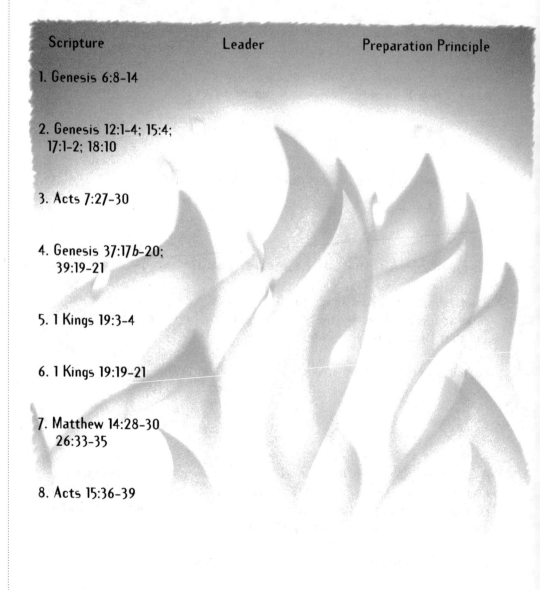

Scripture	Leader	Preparation Principle
1. Genesis 6:8-14		
2. Genesis 12:1-4; 15:4; 17:1-2; 18:10		
3. Acts 7:27-30		
4. Genesis 37:17b-20; 39:19-21		
5. 1 Kings 19:3-4		
6. 1 Kings 19:19-21		
7. Matthew 14:28-30 26:33-35		
8. Acts 15:36-39		

Review these preparation circumstances by matching the leader with the experience:

Paul   Had a servant heart; followed a mentor's leadership

Noah   Disappointed by friends

Moses   Walked with God when others were sinful

Peter   Self-confidence led to failure.

Abraham   Faith tested by God's timetable

Elisha   Spent years in a desert

Elijah   Endured difficult circumstances

Joseph   Discouraged and afraid

List each of the above preparation experiences and explain how God can use it to prepare a man or woman for ministry.

1.

2.

3.

4.

5.

6.

7.

8.

Circle in the list any experience you feel God is presently using in your life to mature you spiritually and prepare you for ministry in His kingdom work.

[1] Henry Blackaby, Henry Brandt, with Kerry L Skinner, *The Power of the Call* (Nashville: Broadman & Holman Publishers, 1997), 223.
[2] Ibid., 224.
[3] Ibid.
[4] Ibid., 226.
[5] Ibid., 227.
[6] Ibid., 228.
[7] Ibid., 230.
[8] Ibid., 231.
[9] Ibid., 234.
[10] Frank Damazio, *The Making of a Leader* (Portland, OR; Bible Temple Publishing, 1988), 171.

DECISION/
VOCATIONAL COMMITMENT CARD

FORM - 285 (Rev. 12-96)

RETURN TO ADDRESS ON OPPOSITE SIDE IF THIS IS A VOCATIONAL DECISION

PLEASE PRINT

First Name _____ | MI ___ | Last Name _____ (Preferred Name) | Social Security Number ___ - ___ - ___

Home Address _____ | City _____ | State ___ | Zip Code ___ | Home Telephone (___) ___

Birth Date (Mon/Day/Year) _____
| HS/College Graduation Year _____ | ☐ Male ☐ Female | ☐ Anglo ☐ Asian ☐ Black ☐ Other ☐ Hispanic | Language Spoken Other Than English ☐ Spanish ☐ French ☐ Japanese ☐ Chinese ☐ Other _____

If full time college student — include college mailing address:

Address _____ | Name of High School _____

City _____ State ___ Zip ___ | ☐ Single-Never Married   ☐ Divorced   ☐ Married   ☐ Widowed

Check Vocational area(s) in which you are interested.
☐ Church Staff   ☐ Home Missions | Minister's Name _____
☐ Associational Missions ☐ Foreign Missions | Home Church _____
☐ State Missions | Church Address _____

Decision:
☐ I receive Christ as my Savior and Lord. | City _____ State ___ Zip ___
☐ I reaffirm my commitment to make Christ the Lord of my life (rededication).
☐ I feel definitely God is leading me toward a ministry vocation. | Campus/Youth Minister's Name _____
☐ I want to explore opportunities in ministry vocations. | Address _____
☐ I am interested in volunteer missions opportunities. | City _____ State ___ Zip ___
☐ Other _____

Send the completed page to: Vocational Guidance, MSN 166, 127 Ninth Avenue, North, Nashville, TN 37234-0166

Notes

CHRISTIAN GROWTH STUDY PLAN

Preparing Christians to Serve

In the **Christian Growth Study Plan (formerly Church Study Course),** this book
God's Call: The Cornerstone of Effective Ministry is a resource for course credit in three Leadership and
Skill Development diploma plans. To receive credit, read the book, complete the learning activities,
show your work to your pastor, a staff member or church leader, then complete the following information.
This page may be duplicated. Send the completed page to:

Christian Growth Study Plan
127 Ninth Avenue, North, MSN 117
Nashville, TN 37234-0117
FAX: (615)251-5067

For information about the Christian Growth Study Plan, refer to the current Christian Growth Study Plan Catalog.
Your church office may have a copy. If not, request a free copy from the Christian Growth Study Plan
office (615/251-2525).

PARTICIPANT INFORMATION

Social Security Number (USA ONLY)	Personal CGSP Number*	Date of Birth (MONTH, DAY, YEAR)
– –	–	– –

Name (First, Middle, Last)   Home Phone
☐ Mr. ☐ Miss
☐ Mrs. ☐

Address (Street, Route, or P.O. Box)	City, State, or Province	Zip/Postal Code

CHURCH INFORMATION

Church Name

Address (Street, Route, or P.O. Box)	City, State, or Province	Zip/Postal Code

CHANGE REQUEST ONLY

☐ Former Name

☐ Former Address	City, State, or Province	Zip/Postal Code

☐ Former Church	City, State, or Province	Zip/Postal Code

Signature of Pastor, Conference Leader, or Other Church Leader	Date

*New participants are requested but not required to give SS# and date of birth. Existing participants, please give CGSP# when using SS# for the first time.
Thereafter, only one ID# is required. **Mail to:** Christian Growth Study Plan, 127 Ninth Ave., North, Nashville, TN 37234-0117. Fax: (615)251-5067